Women of

by Benjamin Brawley

CONTENTS

I. Introduction.--The Negro Woman in American Life.

II. Harriet Tubman.

III. Nora Gordon.

IV. Meta Warrick Fuller.

V. Mary McLeod Bethune.

VI. Mary Church Terrell.

THE FIRESIDE SCHOOLS

The work of the Fireside Schools was begun in 1884 by Joanna P. Moore, who was born in Clarion County, Pennsylvania, September 26, 1832, and who died in Selma, Alabama, April 15, 1916. For fifty years Miss Moore was well known as an earnest worker for the betterment of the Negro people of the South. Beginning in the course of the Civil War, at Island No. 10, in November, 1863, she gave herself untiringly to the work to which she felt called. In 1864 she ministered to a group of people at Helena, Arkansas. In 1868 she went to Lauderdale, Mississippi, to help the Friends in an orphan asylum. While she was at one time left temporarily in charge of the institution cholera broke out, and eleven children died within one week; but she remained at her post until the fury of the plague was abated. She spent nine years in the vicinity of New Orleans, reading the Bible to those who could not read, writing letters in search of lost ones, and especially caring for the helpless old women that she met. In 1877 the Woman's American Baptist Home Mission Society gave her its first commission.

The object of the Fireside Schools is to secure the daily prayerful study of God's word by having this read to parents and children together; to teach parents and children, husbands and wives, their respective duties one to another; to supply homes with good reading matter; and also to inculcate temperance, industry, neighborly helpfulness, and greater attention to the work of the church. The publication of Hope, the organ of the Fireside Schools, was begun in 1885. Closely associated with the Schools are the Bible Bands, a single band consisting of any two or three people in the same church or neighborhood who meet to review the lessons in Hope and to report and plan Christian work. All the activities are under the general supervision of the Woman's American Baptist Home Mission Society, though the special Fireside School headquarters are at 612 Gay Street, Nashville, Tennessee. The present work is dedicated to the memory of Joanna P. Moore, and to the wives and mothers and sisters, now happily numbered by the thousands, who are engaged in the work of the Fireside Schools.

I.

INTRODUCTION.

The Negro Woman in American Life

In the history of the Negro race in America no more heroic work has been done than that performed by the Negro woman. The great responsibilities of life have naturally drifted to the men; but who can measure the patience, the love, the self-sacrifice of those who in a more humble way have labored for their people and even in the midst of war striven most earnestly to keep the home-fires burning? Even before emancipation a strong character had made herself felt in more than one community; and to-day, whether in public life, social service, education, missions, business, literature, music, or even the professions and scholarship, the Negro woman is making her way and reflecting credit upon a race that for so many years now has been struggling to the light.

It was but natural that those should first become known who were interested in the uplift of the race. If we except such an unusual and specially gifted spirit as Phillis Wheatley, we shall find that those who most impressed the American public before the Civil War were the ones who best identified themselves with the general struggle for freedom. Outstanding was the famous lecturer, Sojourner Truth. This remarkable woman was born of slave parents in the state of New York about 1798. She recalled vividly in her later years the cold, damp cellar-room in which slept the slaves of the family to which she belonged, and where she was taught by her mother to repeat the Lord's Prayer and to trust God at all times. When in the course of the process of gradual emancipation in New York she became legally free in 1827, her master refused to comply with the law. She left, but was pursued and found. Rather than have her go back, however, a friend paid for her services for the rest of the year. Then there came an evening when, searching for one of her children that had been stolen and sold, she found herself without a resting-place for the night. A Quaker family, however, gave her lodging. Afterwards she went to New York City, joined a Methodist church, and worked hard to improve her condition. Later, having decided to leave New York for a lecture tour through the East, she made a small bundle of her belongings and informed a friend that her name was no longer Isabella, as she had been known, but Sojourner. Afterwards, as she herself said, finding that she needed two names she adopted Truth, because it was intended that she should declare the truth to the people. She went on her way, lecturing to people wherever she found them assembled and being entertained in many aristocratic homes. She was entirely untaught in the schools, but tall and of commanding presence, original, witty, and always suggestive. The stories told about her are numberless; but she was ever moved by an abiding trust in God, and she counted among her friends many of the most distinguished Americans of her time. By her tact and her gift of song she kept down ridicule, and by her fervor and faith she won many friends for the anti-slavery cause.

It was impossible of course for any single woman to carry on the tradition of such a character as Sojourner Truth. She belonged to a distinct epoch in the country's history, one in which the rights of the Negro and the rights of woman in general were frequently discussed on the same platform; and she passed--so far as her greatest influence was concerned--with her epoch. In more recent years those women who have represented the race before the larger public have been persons of more training and culture, though it has been practically impossible for any one to equal the native force and wit of Sojourner Truth. Outstanding in recent years have been Mrs. Booker T. Washington and Mrs. Mary Church Terrell. The spread of culture, however, and the general force of the social emphasis have more and more led those who were interested in social betterment to come together so that there might be the greater effect from united effort. Thus we have had developing in almost all of our cities and towns various clubs working for the good of the race, whether the immediate aim was literary culture, an orphanage, an old folks' home, the protection of working girls, or something else similarly noble. Prominent among the pioneers in such work were Mrs. Josephine St. Pierre Ruffin, of Boston, and Mrs. John T. Cook, of Washington, D. C. No one can record exactly how much has been accomplished by these organizations; in fact, the clubs range all the way in effectiveness from one that is a dominating force in its town to one that is struggling to get started. The result of the work, however, would in any case sum up with an astonishing total. A report from Illinois, fairly representative of the stronger work, mentioned the following activities: "The Cairo hospital, fostered and under the supervision of the Yates Club of Cairo; the Anna Field Home for Girls, Peoria; Lincoln Old Folks' and Orphans' Home, founded by Mrs. Eva Monroe and assisted by the Women's Club of Springfield; the Home for Aged and Infirm Colored People, Chicago, founded by Mrs. Gabrella Smith and others; the Amanda Smith Orphans' Home, Harvey; the Phillis Wheatley Home for Wage-Earning Girls, of Chicago." In Alabama the State Federation of Colored Women's Clubs has established and is supporting a reformatory at Mt. Meigs for Negro boys, and the women are very enthusiastic about the work. A beautiful and well ordered home for Negro girls was established a few years ago in Virginia. Of the White Rose Mission of New York we are told that it "has done much good. A large number of needy ones have found shelter within its doors and have been able to secure work of all kinds. This club has a committee to meet the incoming steamers from the South and see that young women entering the city as strangers are directed to proper homes." All such work is touching in its tenderness and effectiveness. The National Association of Colored

Women's Clubs was founded in 1896. The organization has become stronger and stronger until it is now a powerful and effective one with hundreds of members. One of its recent activities has been the purchase of the home of Frederick Douglass at Anacostia, D. C.

In education, church life, and missions--special forms of social service--we have only to look around us to see what the Negro woman is accomplishing. Not only is she bearing the brunt of common school education for the race; in more than one instance a strong character, moved to do something, has started on a career of success a good secondary or industrial school. Representative are the Voorhees Normal and Industrial School, at Denmark, S. C., founded by Elizabeth C. Wright; the Daytona Normal and Industrial Institute for Negro Girls, founded by Mrs. M. M. Bethune; and the Mt. Meigs Institute, Mt. Meigs, Alabama, founded by Miss Cornelia Bowen. Noteworthy for its special missionary emphasis is the National Training School of Washington, of which Miss Nannie H. Burroughs is the head. One of the most important recent developments in education has been the appointment of a number of young women as supervisors in county schools under the terms of the will of Anna T. Jeanes, a Quaker lady of Philadelphia who left a considerable sum of money for the improvement of the rural schools of the South. In church work we all know the extent to which women have had to bear the burden not only of the regular activities but also of the numerous "rallies" that still so unfortunately afflict our churches. Deserving of special mention in connection with social service is the work of those who have labored under the auspices of the Young Women's Christian Association, which has done so much for the moral well-being of the great camps in the war. In foreign mission work one of the educational institutions sustained primarily by Northern Baptist agencies--Spelman Seminary--stands out with distinct prominence. Not only has Spelman sent to Africa several of her daughters from this country, the first one being Nora Gordon in 1889; she has also educated several who have come to her from Africa, the first being Lena Clark, and for these the hope has ever been that they would return to their own country for their largest and most mature service.

In the realm of business the Negro woman has stood side by side with her husband in the rise to higher things. In almost every instance in which a man has prospered, investigation will show that his advance was very largely due to the faith, the patience, and the untiring effort of his wife. Dr. B. T. Washington, in his book The Negro in Business, gave several examples. One of the outstanding instances was in the story of Junius G. Groves, famous potato grower of Edwardsville, Kansas. This man moved from his original home in Kentucky to Kansas at the time of the well-known "Exodus" of 1879, a migration movement which was even more voluntary on the part of the Negro than the recent removal to the North on the part of so many, this latter movement being in so many ways a result of war conditions. Mr. Groves in course of time became a man of large responsibilities and means. It is most interesting, however, to go back to his early days of struggle. We read as follows: "Soon after getting the crop planted Mr. Groves decided to marry. When he reached this decision he had but seventy-five cents in cash, and had to borrow enough to satisfy the demands of the law. But he knew well the worth and common sense of the woman he was to marry. She was as poor in worldly goods as himself; but their poverty did not discourage them in their plans. * * * * During the whole season they worked with never-tiring energy, early and late; with the result that when the crop had been harvested and all debts paid they had cleared $125. Notwithstanding their lack of many necessaries of life, to say nothing of comforts, they decided to invest $50 of their earnings in a lot in Kansas City, Kansas. They paid $25 for a milk cow, and kept the remaining $50 to be used in the making of another crop." In the course of a few years Mr. Groves, with the help of his wife, now the mother of a large family, gathered in one year hundreds of thousands of bushels of white potatoes, surpassing all other growers in the world. Similarly was the success of E. C. Berry, a hotel-keeper of Athens, Ohio, due to his wife. "At night, after his guests had fallen asleep, it was his custom to go around and gather up their clothes and take them to his wife, who would add buttons which were lacking, repair rents, and press the garments, after which Mr. Berry would replace them in the guests' rooms. Guests who had received such treatment returned again and brought their friends with them." In course of time Mr. and Mrs. Berry came to own the leading hotel in Athens, one of fifty rooms and of special favor with commercial travelers.

Such examples could be multiplied indefinitely. It is not only in such spheres that the worth of the Negro woman has been shown, however. Daily, in thousands of homes, in little stores and on humble farms, effort just as heroic has been exerted, though the result is not always so evident. On their own initiative also women are now engaging in large enterprises. The most conspicuous example of material success is undoubtedly Mme. C. J. Walker, of the Mme. C. J. Walker Manufacturing Company, of Indianapolis and New York, a business that is now conducted on a large scale and in accordance with the best business methods of America. Important also in this connection is the very great contribution that Negro women--very often those without education and opportunity--are making in the ordinary industrial life of the country. According to the census of 1910, 1,047,146, or 52 per cent. of those at work, were either farmers or farm laborers, and 28 per cent. more were either cooks or washerwomen. In other words, a total of exactly 80 per cent. were doing some of the hardest and at the same time some of the most necessary work in our home and industrial life. These are workers whose worth has never been fully appreciated by the larger public, and who needed the heavy demands of the great war to call attention to the actual value of the service they were rendering.

The changes in fact brought about within the last few years, largely as a result of war conditions, are remarkable. As Mary E. Jackson, writing in the Crisis, has said: "Indiana reports [Negro women] in glass works; in Ohio they are found on the night shifts of glass works; they have gone into the pottery works in Virginia; wood-working plants and lumber yards have called for their help in Tennessee." She also quotes Rachel S. Gallagher, of Cleveland, Ohio, as saying of the Negro women in that city: "We find them on power sewing-machines, making caps, waists, bags, and mops; we find them doing pressing and various hand operations in these same shops. They are employed in knitting factories as winders, in a number of laundries on mangles of every type, and in sorting and marking. They are in paper box factories doing both hand and machine work, in button factories on the button machines, in packing houses packing meat, in railroad yards wiping and cleaning engines, and doing sorting in railroad shops. One of our workers recently found two colored girls on a knotting machine in a bed spring factory, putting the knots in the wire springs."

In the professions, such as medicine and law, and in scholarship as well, the Negro woman has blazed a path. One year after Oberlin College in Ohio was founded in 1833, thirty years before the issuing of the Emancipation Proclamation, the trustees took the advanced ground of admitting Negro men and women on equal terms with other students. Of the Northern colleges and universities Oberlin still leads in the number of its Negro women graduates, but in recent years other such institutions as Radcliffe, Wellesley, Columbia, and Chicago have been represented in an increasing number by those who have finished their work creditably and even with distinction in many instances. More and more each year are young women at these institutions going forward to the attainment of the higher scholastic degrees. In connection with medicine we recall the work in the war of the Negro woman in the related profession of nursing. It was only after considerable discussion that she was given a genuine opportunity in Red Cross work, but she at once vindicated herself. In the legal profession she has not only been admitted to practice in various places, but has also been appointed to public office. It must be understood that such positions as those just remarked are not secured without a struggle, but all told they indicate that the race through its womanhood is more and more taking part in the general life of the country.

In keeping with the romantic quality of the race it was but natural that from the first there should have been special effort at self-expression in literature, music, and other forms of art. The first Negro woman to strike the public imagination was Phillis Wheatley, who even as a young girl wrote acceptable verse. Her Poems on Various Subjects published in 1773 at once attracted attention, and it was fitting that the first Negro woman to become distinguished in America should be one of outstanding piety and nobility of soul. Just a few years before the Civil War Frances Ellen Watkins, better known as Mrs. F. E. W. Harper, entered upon her career as a writer of popular poetry. At the present time attention centers especially upon Mrs. Georgia Douglas Johnson, who early in 1918 produced in The Heart of a Woman a little volume of delicate and poignantly beautiful verse, and from whom greater and greater things are expected, as she not only has the temperament of an artist but has also undergone a period of severe training in her chosen field. In the wider field of prose--including especially stories, essays, and sketches--Mrs. Alice Moore Dunbar-Nelson is prominent. In 1899 she produced The Goodness of St. Rocque, and other stories, and since then has continued her good work in various ways. The whole field of literature is a wide one, one naturally appealing to many of the younger women, and one that with all its difficulties and lack of financial return does offer some genuine reward to the candidate who is willing to work hard and who does not seek a short cut to fame.

In music the race has produced more women of distinction than in any other field. This was natural, for the Negro voice is world famous. The pity is that all too frequently some of the most capable young women have not had the means to cultivate their talents and hence have fallen by the wayside. Some day it is to be hoped that a great philanthropist will endow a real conservatory at which such persons may find some genuine opportunity and encouragement in their development in their days of struggle. In spite of all the difficulties, however, there have been singers who have risen to very high things in their art. Even before the Civil War the race produced one of the first rank in Elizabeth Taylor Greenfield, who came into prominence in 1851. This artist, born in Mississippi, was taken to Philadelphia and there cared for by a Quaker lady. The young woman did not soon reveal her gift to her friend, thinking that it might be frowned upon as something too worldly. Her guardian learned of it by accident, however, and one day surprised her by asking, "Elizabeth, is it true that thee can sing?" "Yes," replied the young woman in confusion. "Let me hear thee." And Elizabeth sang; and her friend, realizing that she had a voice of the first quality, proceeded to give her the best instruction that it was possible to get. Elizabeth Taylor Greenfield had a marvelous voice embracing twenty-seven notes, reaching from the sonorous bass of a baritone to the highest soprano. A voice with a range of more than three octaves naturally attracted much attention in both England and America, and comparisons with Jenny Lind, then at the height of her great fame, were frequent. In the next generation arose Madame Selika, a cultured singer of the first rank, and one who by her arias and operatic work generally, as well as by her mastery of language, won great success on the continent of Europe as well as in England and America. The careers of some later singers are so recent as to be still fresh in the public memory; some in fact may still be heard. It was in 1887 that Flora Batson entered on the period of her greatest success. She was a ballad singer and her work at its best was of the sort that sends an audience into the wildest enthusiasm. In a series of temperance meetings in New York she sang for ninety consecutive nights, with never-failing effect, one song, "Six Feet of Earth Make Us All One Size." Her voice exhibited a compass of three octaves, but even more important than its range was its remarkable sympathetic quality. Early in the last decade of the century appeared also Mrs. Sissieretta Jones, whose voice at once commanded attention as one of unusual richness and volume, and as one exhibiting especially the plaintive quality ever present in the typical Negro voice.

At the present time there are several promising singers; and there are also those who in various ways are working for the general advancement of the race in music. Mrs. E. Azalia Hackley, for some years prominent as a concert soprano, has recently given her time most largely to the work of teaching and showing the capabilities of the Negro voice. Possessed of a splendid musical temperament, she has enjoyed the benefit of three years of foreign study and generally inspired many younger singers or performers. Prominent among many excellent pianists is Mrs. Hazel Harrison Anderson, who also has studied much abroad and who has appeared in many noteworthy recitals. Mrs. Maud Cuney Hare, of Boston, a concert pianist, has within the last few years given several excellent lecture-recitals dealing with Afro-American music.

As between painting and sculpture the women of the race have shown a decided preference for sculpture. While there are some students of promise, no woman has as yet achieved distinction on work of really professional quality in the realm of painting. On the other hand there have been three or four sculptors of genuine merit. As early as 1865 Edmonia Lewis began to attract attention by her busts of prominent people. Within the last few years the work of Mrs. May Howard Jackson, of Washington, has attracted the attention of the discerning; and that of Mrs. Meta Warrick Fuller is reserved for special comment.

Any such review as this naturally has its limitations. We can indicate only a few of the outstanding individuals here and there. At least enough has been said, however, to show that the Negro woman is making her way at last into every phase of noble endeavor. In the pages that follow we shall attempt to set forth at somewhat greater length the life and work of a few of those whose achievement has been most signal and whose interest in their sisters has been unfailing.

IN MEMORY OF

HARRIET TUBMAN

BORN A SLAVE IN MARYLAND ABOUT 1821 DIED IN AUBURN, N.Y. MARCH 10TH, 1913

CALLED THE "MOSES" OF HER PEOPLE. DURING THE CIVIL WAR, WITH RARE COURAGE, SHE LED OVER THREE HUNDRED NEGROES UP FROM SLAVERY TO FREEDOM, AND RENDERED INVALUABLE SERVICE AS NURSE AND SPY.

WITH IMPLICIT TRUST IN GOD SHE BRAVED EVERY DANGER AND OVERCAME EVERY OBSTACLE, WITHAL SHE POSSESSED EXTRAORDINARY FORESIGHT AND JUDGMENT SO THAT SHE TRUTHFULLY SAID--

"ON MY UNDERGROUND RAILROAD I NEBBER RUN MY TRAIN OFF DE TRACK AND I NEBBER LOS' A PASSENGER."

* * * * *

THIS TABLET IS ERECTED BY THE CITIZENS OF AUBURN ?914?
Used through courtesy of John Williams, Inc., Bronze Foundry and Iron Works, New York, N. Y.]

II.

HARRIET TUBMAN[A]

Greatest of all the heroines of anti-slavery was Harriet Tubman. This brave woman not only escaped from bondage herself, but afterwards made nineteen distinct trips to the South, especially to Maryland, and altogether aided more than three hundred souls in escaping from their fetters.

Araminta Ross, better known by the Christian name Harriet that she adopted, and her married name of Tubman, was born about 1821 in Dorchester County, on the eastern shore of Maryland, the daughter of Benjamin Ross and Harriet Greene, both of whom were slaves, but who were privileged to be able to live their lives in a state of singular fidelity. Harriet had ten brothers and sisters, not less than three of whom she rescued from slavery; and in 1857, at great risk to herself, she also took away to the North her aged father and mother.

When Harriet was not more than six years old she was taken away from her mother and sent ten miles away to learn the trade of weaving. Among other things she was set to the task of watching muskrat traps, which work compelled her to wade much in water. Once she was forced to work when she was already ill with the measles. She became very sick, and her mother now persuaded her master to let the girl come home for a while.

Soon after Harriet entered her teens she suffered a misfortune that embarrassed her all the rest of her life. She had been hired out as a field hand. It was the fall of the year and the slaves were busy at such tasks as husking corn and cleaning up wheat. One of them ran away. He was found. The overseer swore that he should be whipped and called on Harriet and some others that happened to be near to help tie him. She refused, and as the slave made his escape she placed herself in a door to help to stop pursuit of him. The overseer caught up a two-pound weight and threw it at the fugitive; but it missed its mark and struck Harriet a blow on the head that was almost fatal. Her skull was broken and from this resulted a pressure on her brain which all her life left her subject to fits of somnolency. Sometimes these would come upon her in the midst of a conversation or any task at which she might be engaged; then after a while the spell would pass and she could go on as before.

After Harriet recovered sufficiently from her blow she lived for five or six years in the home of one John Stewart, working at first in the house but afterwards hiring her time. She performed the most arduous labor in order to get the fifty or sixty dollars ordinarily exacted of a woman in her situation. She drove oxen, plowed, cut wood, and did many other such things. With her firm belief in Providence, in her later years she referred to this work as a blessing in disguise as it gave her the firm constitution necessary for the trials and hardships that were before her. Sometimes she worked for her father, who was a timber inspector and superintended the cutting and hauling of large quantities of timber for the Baltimore ship-yards. Her regular task in this employment was the cutting of half a cord of wood a day.

About 1844 Harriet was married to a free man named John Tubman. She had no children. Two years after her escape in 1849 she traveled back to Maryland for her husband, only to find him married to another woman and no longer caring to live with her. She felt the blow keenly, but did not despair and more and more gave her thought to what was to be the great work of her life.

It was not long after her marriage that Harriet began seriously to consider the matter of escape from bondage. Already in her mind her people were the Israelites in the land of Egypt, and far off in the North somewhere was the land of Canaan. In 1849 the master of her plantation died, and word passed around that at any moment she and two of her brothers were to be sold to the far South. Harriet, now twenty-four years old, resolved to put her long cherished dreams into effect. She held a consultation with her brothers and they decided to start with her at once, that very night, for the North. She could not go away, however, without giving some intimation of her purpose to the friends she was leaving behind. As it was not advisable for slaves to be seen too much talking together, she went among her old associates singing as follows:

When dat ar ol' chariot comes I'm gwine to leabe you; I'm boun' for de Promised Land; Frien's, I'm gwine to leabe you.

I'm sorry, frien's, to leabe you; Farewell! oh, farewell! But I'll meet you in de mornin'; Farewell! oh, farewell!

I'll meet you in de mornin' When you reach de Promised Land; On de oder side of Jordan, For I'm boun' for de Promised Land.

The brothers started with her; but the way was unknown, the North was far away, and they were constantly in terror of recapture. They turned back, and Harriet, after watching their retreating forms, again fixed her eyes on the north star. "I had reasoned dis out in my min'," said she; "there was one of two things I had a right to, liberty or death. If I could not have one, I would have de other, for no man should take me alive. I would fight for my liberty as long as my strength lasted, and when de time came for me to go, the Lord would let them take me."

"And so without money, and without friends," says Mrs. Bradford, "she started on through unknown regions; walking by night, hiding by day, but always conscious of an invisible pillar of cloud by day, and of fire by night, under the guidance of which she journeyed or rested. Without knowing whom to trust, or how near the pursuers might be, she carefully felt her way, and by her native cunning, or by God-given wisdom she managed to apply to the right people for food, and sometimes for shelter; though often her bed was only the cold ground, and her watchers the stars of night. After many long and weary days of travel, she found that she had passed the magic line which then divided the land of bondage from the land of freedom." At length she came to Philadelphia, where she found work and the opportunity to earn a little money. It was at this time, in 1851, after she had been employed for some months, that she went back to Maryland for her husband only to find that he had not been true.

In December, 1850, she had visited Baltimore and brought away a sister and two children. A few months afterwards she took away a brother and two other men. In December, 1851, she led out a party of eleven, among them being another brother and his wife. With these she journeyed to Canada, for the Fugitive Slave Law was now in force and, as she quaintly said, there was no safety except "under the paw of the British Lion." The winter, however, was hard on the poor fugitives, who unused to the climate of Canada, had to chop wood in the forests in the snow. Often they were frost-bitten, hungry, and almost always poorly clad. But Harriet was caring for them. She kept house for her brother, and the fugitives boarded with her. She begged for them and prayed for them, and somehow got them through the hard winter. In the spring she returned to the States, as usual working in hotels and families as a cook. In 1852 she once more went to Maryland, this time bringing away nine fugitives.

It must not be supposed that those who started on the journey northward were always strong-spirited characters. The road was rough and attended by dangers innumerable. Sometimes the fugitives grew faint-hearted and wanted to turn back. Then would come into play the pistol that Harriet always carried with her. "Dead niggers tell no tales," said she, pointing it at them; "you go on or die!" By this heroic method she forced many to go onward and win the goal of freedom.

Unfailing was Harriet Tubman's confidence in God. A customary form of prayer for her was, "O Lord, you've been with me in six troubles; be with me in the seventh." On one of her journeys she came with a party of fugitives to the home of a Negro who had more than once assisted her and whose house was one of the regular stations on the so-called Underground Railroad. Leaving her party a little distance away Harriet went to the door and gave the peculiar rap that was her regular signal. Not meeting with a ready response, she knocked several times. At length a window was raised and a white man demanded roughly what she wanted. When Harriet asked for her friend she was informed that he had been obliged to leave for assisting Negroes. The situation was dangerous. Day was breaking and something had to be done at once. A prayer revealed to Harriet a place of refuge. Outside of the town she remembered that there was a little island in a swamp, with much tall grass upon it. Hither she conducted her party, carrying in a basket two babies that had been drugged. All were cold and hungry in the wet grass; still Harriet prayed and waited for deliverance. How relief came she never knew; she felt that it was not necessarily her business to know. After they had waited through the day, however, at dusk there came slowly along the pathway on the edge of the swamp a man clad in the garb of a Quaker. He seemed to be talking to himself, but Harriet's sharp ears caught the words: "My wagon stands in the barnyard of the next farm across the way. The horse is in the stable; the harness hangs on a nail;" and then the man was gone. When night came Harriet stole forth to the place designated, and found not only the wagon but also abundant provisions in it, so that the whole party was soon on its way rejoicing. In the next town dwelt a Quaker whom Harriet knew and who readily took charge of the horse and wagon for her.

Naturally the work of such a woman could not long escape the attention of the abolitionists. She became known to Thomas Garrett, the great-hearted Quaker of Wilmington, who aided not less than three thousand fugitives to escape, and also to Grit Smith, Wendell Phillips, William H. Seward, F. B. Sanborn, and many other notable men interested in the emancipation of the Negro. From time to time she was supplied with money, but she never spent this for her own use, setting it aside in case of need on the next one of her journeys. In her earlier years, however, before she became known, she gave of her own slender means for the work.

Between 1852 and 1857 she made but one or two journeys, because of the increasing vigilance of slaveholders and the Fugitive Slave Law. Great rewards were offered for her capture and she was several times on the point of being taken, but always escaped by her shrewd wit and what she considered warnings from heaven. While she was intensely practical, she was also a most firm believer in dreams. In 1857 she made her most venturesome journey, this time taking with her to the North her old parents who were no longer able to walk such distances as she was forced to go by night. Accordingly she had to hire a wagon for them, and it took all her ingenuity to get them through Maryland and Delaware. At length, however, she got them to Canada, where they spent the winter. As the climate was too rigorous, however, she afterwards brought them down to New York, and settled them in a home in Auburn, N. Y., that she had purchased on very reasonable terms from Secretary Seward. Somewhat later a mortgage on the place had to be lifted and Harriet now made a noteworthy visit to Boston, returning with a handsome sum toward the payment of her debt. At this time she met John Brown more than once, seems to have learned something of his plans, and after the raid at Harper's Ferry and the execution of Brown she glorified him as a hero, her veneration even becoming religious. Her last visit to Maryland was made in December, 1860, and in spite of the agitated condition of the country and the great watchfulness of slaveholders she brought away with her seven fugitives, one of them an infant.

After the war Harriet Tubman made Auburn her home, establishing there a refuge for aged Negroes. She married again, so that she is sometimes referred to as Harriet Tubman Davis. She died at a very advanced age March 10, 1913. On Friday, June 12, 1914, a tablet in her honor was unveiled at the Auditorium in Albany. It was provided by the Cayuga County Historical Association, Dr. Booker T. Washington was the chief speaker of the occasion, and the ceremonies were attended by a great crowd of people.

The tributes to this heroic woman were remarkable. Wendell Phillips said of her: "In my opinion there are few captains, perhaps few colonels, who have done more for the loyal cause since the war began, and few men who did before that time more for the colored race than our fearless and most sagacious friend, Harriet." F. B. Sanborn wrote that what she did "could scarcely be credited on the best authority." William H. Seward, who labored, though unsuccessfully, to get a pension for her granted by Congress, consistently praised her noble spirit. Abraham Lincoln gave her ready audience and lent a willing ear to whatever she had to say. Frederick Douglass wrote to her: "The difference between us is very marked. Most that I have done and suffered in the service of our cause has been in public, and I have received much encouragement at every step of the way. You, on the other hand, have labored in a private way. I have wrought in the day--you in the night. I have had the applause of the crowd and the satisfaction that comes of being approved by the multitude, while the most that you have done has been witnessed by a few trembling, scarred, and footsore bondmen and women, whom you have led out of the house of bondage, and whose heartfelt 'God bless you' has been your only reward."

Of such mould was Harriet Tubman, philanthropist and patriot, bravest and noblest of all the heroines of freedom.

FOOTNOTE:

[A] While this sketch is drawn from various sources, I feel specially indebted to Sarah H. Bradford's "Harriet, the Moses of Her People." This valuable work in turn includes a scholarly article taken from the "Boston Commonwealth" of 1863 and loaned to Mrs. Bradford by F. R. Sanborn. This article is really the foundation of the sketch.--B. B.

III.

NORA GORDON

This is the story of a young woman who had not more than ordinary advantages, but who in our own day by her love for Christ and her zeal in his service was swept from her heroic labor into martyrdom.

When Nora Gordon went from Spelman Seminary as a missionary to the Congo, she had the hope that in some little way she might be used for the furtherance of the Master's kingdom. She could hardly have foreseen that she would start in her beloved school a glorious tradition; and still less could she have seen the marvellous changes taking place in the Africa of the present. She had boundless faith, however,--faith in God and in the ultimate destiny of her people. In that faith she lived, and for that faith she died.

Nora Antonia Gordon was born in Columbus, Georgia, August 25, 1866. After receiving her early education in the public schools of La Grange, in the fall of 1882 she came to Spelman Seminary. It was not long before her life became representative of the transforming power of Christianity. Being asked, "Do you love Christ?" she answered "Yes"; but when there came the question, "Are you a Christian?" she replied "No." It was not long, however, before she gained firmer faith, and two months after her entrance at Spelman she was definitely converted. Now followed seven years of intense activity and growth--of study, of summer teaching, of talks before temperance societies, of service of any possible sort for the Master. She brought to Christ every girl who was placed to room with her. A classmate afterwards testified of her that the girls always regarded Nora somewhat differently from the others. She was the counsellor of her friends, ever ready with sweet words of comfort, and yet ever a cheerful companion. In one home in which she lived for a while she asked the privilege of having prayer. The man of the house at first refused to kneel and the woman seemed not interested. In course of time, however, the wife was won and then the man also knelt. At another time she wrote, "Twenty-six of my scholars were baptized to-day;" and a little later she said, "Ten more have been added."

In 1885 Nora Gordon completed her course in the Industrial Department, in 1886 the Elementary Normal, and in 1888 the Higher Normal Course. Her graduation essay was on the rather old and sophomoric subject, "The Influence of Woman on National Character;" but in the intensity of her convictions and her words there was nothing ordinary. She said in part: "Let no woman feel that life to her means simply living; but let her rather feel that she has a special mission assigned her, which none other of God's creatures can perform. It may be that she is placed in some rude little hut as mother and wife; if so, she can dignify her position by turning every hut into a palace, and bringing not only her own household, but the whole community, into the sunlight of God's love. Such women are often unnoticed by the world in general, and do not receive the appreciation due them; yet we believe such may be called God's chosen agents." Finally, "we feel that woman is under a twofold obligation to consecrate her whole being to Christ. Our people are to be educated and christianized and the heathen brought home to God. Woman must take the lead in this great work."

After her graduation in 1888 Nora Gordon was appointed to teach in the public schools of Atlanta. She soon resigned this work, however, in the contemplation of the great mission of her life. The secretary of the Society of the West wrote to Spelman to inquire if there was any one who could go to assist Miss Fleming, a missionary at work in Palabala in the Congo. Four names were sent, and the choice of the board was Nora A. Gordon. The definite appointment came in January, 1889. On Sunday evening, February 17, an impressive missionary service was held in the chapel at Spelman. Interesting items were given by the students with reference to the slave-trade in East Africa and the efforts being made for its suppression, also with reference to Mohammedanism, the spiritual awakening among the Zulus, and the mission stations established, especially those on the Congo. Several letters were read, one from Miss Fleming exciting the most intense interest; and throughout the meeting was the thought that Nora Gordon was also soon to go to Africa. On March 6 a farewell service was held, and attended by a great crowd of people, among them the whole family of the consecrated young woman; and she sailed March 16, 1889.

First of all she went to London, tarrying at the Missionary Training Institute conducted by Rev. and Mrs. H. Grattan Guinness. Under date April 11 she wrote: "It has been so trying to remain here so long waiting. I feel that this is the dear Lord's first lesson to me in patience. I am thankful to say that I feel profited by my stay. * * * * Yesterday coming from the city we saw a number of flags hanging across the street, and among them was the United States flag. Never before did the Stars and Stripes seem so beautiful. I am glad Miss Grover put one in my box. * * * * I do praise God for every step I get nearer to my future home. We expect to sail next Wednesday, April 17, from Rotterdam on the steamer African, Dutch line. We hope to get to the Congo in three weeks."

For two years she labored at Palabala, frequently writing letters home and occasionally sending back to her beloved Spelman a box of curios. Said she of those among whom she worked: "When the people are first gathered into a chapel for school or religious services, it is sad and amusing to see how hard they try to know just what to do, a number sitting with their backs to the preacher or teacher. When the teacher reproves a child, every man, woman, and child feels it his or her duty to yell out too at the offender and tell him to obey the teacher. Often in the midst of a sermon a man in the congregation will call out to the preacher, 'Take away your lies,' or 'We do not believe you,' or 'How can this or that be?' One of the first workers, after speaking to a crowd of heathen, asked them all to close their eyes and bow their heads while he would pray to God. When the missionary had finished his prayer and opened his eyes, every person had stealthily left the place." Then followed a detail of the atrocities in the Congo and of the encounters between the natives and the Belgian officers, and last of all came the pertinent comment: "The Congo missionary's work is twofold. He must civilize, as well as Christianize, the people."

Early in 1891 Nora Gordon, sadly in need of rest and refreshment, went from Palabala for a little stay at Lukungu. Hither had come Clara A. Howard, Spelman's second representative, under appointment of the Woman's Foreign Missionary Society of the East. Lukungu is a station two hundred and twenty miles from the mouth of the Congo, in a populous district, and was the center from which numerous other schools and churches sprang. The work was in charge of Mr. Hoste, an Englishman, who, when Miss Gordon wrote of him in 1894, had spent ten years on the Congo without going home. Other men were associated with him, while the elementary schools, the care of the boys and girls, and work among the women, naturally fell to the women missionaries. A little later in 1891 Nora Gordon left Palabala permanently to engage in the work at Lukungu. Under date September 25 she wrote to her friends back home: "Doubtless Clara has told you of my change to this place. You can not imagine how glad we are to be together here. I have charge of the printing-office and help in the afternoon school. I am well, happy, and am enjoying my work. In the office I have few conveniences and really not the things we need. Mr. Hoste has written the first arithmetic in this language and I am now putting it up. I was obliged to stop work on it to-day because my figures in type gave out, and you know we have no shops in this land. My boys in the office are doing nicely."

Thus she worked on for two years more--hoping, praying, trusting. By 1893 her health was in such condition that it was deemed wise for her to return to America. So she did, and she brought back two native girls with her. All the while, however, her chief thought was upon the work to which she had given herself, and she constantly looked forward to the time when she might be able to go back to Africa. In 1895 she became the wife of Rev. S. C. Gordon, who was connected with the English Baptist Mission at Stanley Pool. She sailed with her husband from Boston in July and reached the Congo again in August. The station was unique. It was an old and well established mission, the center of several others in the surrounding country. It had excellent brick houses, broad avenues and good fruit-trees, and the students were above the average in intelligence. But soon the shadow fell. Nora Gordon herself saw much of the well known Belgian atrocities in the Congo. She saw houses burned and the natives themselves driven out by the state officials. They crossed over into the French Congo; but hither Protestants were not allowed to come to preach to them. In spite of the great heartache, however, and declining health the heroic woman worked on, giving to those for whom she labored her tenderest love. Seven months after the death of her second child a change was again deemed necessary, and she once more turned her face homeward. After two months in Belgium and England she came again to

America, and to Spelman. But her strength was now all spent. She died at Spelman January 26, 1901. She was only thirty-four; but who can measure in years the love and faith, the hope and sorrow, of such a life?

Nora Gordon started a tradition, Spelman's richest heritage. Three other graduates followed her. Clara Howard was in course of time forced by the severe fevers to give up her work, and she now labors at home in the service of her Alma Mater. Ada Jackson became the second wife of Rev. S. C. Gordon and also died in service. Emma B. DeLany was commissioned in 1900 and still labors--in recent years with larger and larger success--in Liberia. Within two or three years of Nora Gordon's return in 1893, moreover, not less than five native African girls had come to Spelman. The spirit still abides, and if the way were just a little clearer doubtless many other graduates would go. Even as it is, however, the blessing to the school has been illimitable.

* * * * *

Such have been the workers, such the pioneers. To what end is the love, the labor--the loneliness, the yearning?

It is now nearly five hundred years since a prince of Portugal began the slave-trade on the west coast of Africa. Within two hundred years all of the leading countries of western Europe had joined in the iniquitous traffic, and when England in 1713 drew up with France the Peace of Utrecht she deemed the slave-trade of such importance that she insisted upon an article that gave her a practical monopoly of it. Before the end of the eighteenth century, however, the voice of conscience began to be heard in England, and science also began to be interested in the great undeveloped continent lying to the South. It remained for the work of David Livingstone, however, in the middle of the nineteenth century really to reveal Africa to the rest of the world. This intrepid explorer and missionary in a remarkable series of journeys not only traversed the continent from the extreme South to Loanda on the West Coast and Quilimane on the East Coast; he not only made known the great lake system of Central Africa; but he left behind him a memory that has blessed everyone who has followed in his steps. Largely as a result of his work and that of his successor, Stanley, a great congress met in Berlin in 1884 for the partition of Africa among the great nations of Europe. Unfortunately the diplomats at this meeting were not actuated by the noble impulses that had moved Livingstone, so that more and more there was evident a mad scramble for territory. France had already gained a firm foothold in the northwest, and England was not only firmly intrenched in the South but had also established a rather undefined protectorate over Egypt. Germany now in 1884 entered the field and in German East Africa, German Southwest Africa, Kamerun, and the smaller territory of Togoland in the West ultimately acquired a total of nearly a million square miles, or one-eleventh of the continent. All of this she lost in the course of the recent great war. Naturally she has desired to regain this land, but at the time of writing (November, 1918) there is no likelihood of her doing so, a distinguished Englishman, Mr. Balfour, the foreign secretary, having declared that under no circumstances can Germany's African colonies be returned to her, as such return would endanger the security of the British empire, and that is to say, the security of the world. This problem is but typical of the larger political questions that press for settlement in the new Africa. Whatever the solution may be, one or two facts stand out clearly. One is that Africa can no longer rest in undisturbed slumber. A terrible war, the most ruinous in the history of humanity, has strained to the utmost the resources of all the great powers of the world. Where so much has been spent it is not to be supposed that the richest, the most fertile, land in the world will indefinitely be allowed to remain undeveloped. Along with material development must go also the education and the spiritual culture of the natives on a scale undreamed of before. In this training such an enlightened country as England will naturally play a leading role, and America too will doubtless be called on to help in more ways than one. It must not be supposed, however, that the task is not one of enormous difficulties. As far as we have advanced in our missionary activities in America, we have hardly made a beginning in the great task of the proper development of Africa. Here are approximately 175,000,000 natives to be trained and Christianized. Let us not make the common mistake of supposing that they are all ignorant and degraded savages. Nothing could be farther from the truth. Many individuals have had the benefit of travel and study in Europe and more and more are themselves appreciating the great problems before their country. It is true, however, that the great mass of the population is yet to be reached. In the general development delicate questions of racial contact are to be answered. Unfortunately, in the attitude of the European colonist toward the native, South Africa has a race problem even more stern than that of our own Southern states. As for religion we not only find paganism and Mohammedanism, but we also see Catholicism arrayed against Protestantism, and perhaps most interesting of all, a definite movement toward the enhancement of a native Ethiopian church, with the motto "Africa for the Africans." Let us add to all this numerous social problems, such as polygamy, the widespread sale of rum, and all the train of African superstition, and we shall see that any one who works in Africa in the new day must not only be a person of keen intelligence and Christian character, but also one with some genuine vision and statesmanship. Workers of this quality, if they can be found, will be needed not by the scores or hundreds, but by the thousands and tens of thousands. No larger mission could come to a young Negro in America trained in Christian study than to make his or her life a part of the redemption of the great fatherland. The salvation of Africa is at once the most pressing problem before either the Negro race or the Kingdom of Christ. Such a worker as we have tried to portray was Nora Gordon. It is to be hoped that not one but thousands like her will arise. Even now we can see the beginning of the fulfilment of the prophecy, "Princes shall come out of Egypt; Ethiopia shall soon stretch out her hands unto God."

IV.

META WARRICK FULLER[B]

The state of Massachusetts has always been famous for its history and literature, and especially rich in tradition is the region around Boston. On one side is Charlestown, visited yearly by thousands who make a pilgrimage to the Bunker Hill Monument. Across the Charles River is Cambridge, the home of Harvard University, and Longfellow, and Lowell, and numerous other men whose work has become a part of the nation's heritage. If one will ride on through Cambridge and North Cambridge and Arlington, he will come to Lexington, where he will find in the little Lexington Common one of the most charming spots of ground in America. Overlooking this he will see the Harrington House, and all around other memorials of the Revolution. Taking the car again and riding about seven miles more he will come to Concord, and here he will catch still more of the flavor of the eighteenth century. Walking from the center of the town down Monument Street (he must walk now; there is no trolley, and a carriage or automobile does not permit one to linger by the wayside), he will come after a while to the Old Manse, once the home of Emerson and of Hawthorne, and then see just around the corner the Concord Bridge and the statue of the Minute Man. There is a new bridge now, one of concrete; the old wooden one, so long beloved, at length became unsafe and had to be replaced. In another direction from the center of the town runs Lexington Road, within about half a mile down which one will see the later homes of Emerson and Hawthorne as well as that of Louisa May Alcott. Near the Alcott House, back among the trees, is a quaint little structure much like a Southern country schoolhouse--the so-called Concord School of Philosophy, in which Emerson once spoke. It is all a beautiful country--beautiful most of all for its unseen glory. One gives himself up to reflection; he muses on Evangeline and the Great Stone Face and on the heroic dead who did not die in vain--until a lumbering truck-car on the road calls him back from it all to the workaday world of men.

It is in this state of Massachusetts, so rich in its tradition, that there resides the subject of the present sketch. About halfway between Boston and Worcester, in the quiet, homelike town of Framingham, on a winding road just off the main street, lives Meta Warrick Fuller, the foremost sculptor of the Negro race.

There are three little boys in the family. They keep their mother very busy; but they also make her very happy. Buttons have to be sewed on and dinners have to be prepared for the children of an artist just as well as for those of other people; and help is not always easy to get. But the father, Dr. S. C.

Fuller, a distinguished physician, is also interested in the boys, so that he too helps, and the home is a happy one.

At the top of the house is a long roomy attic. This is an improvised studio--or, as the sculptor would doubtless say, the workshop. Hither, from the busy work of the morning, comes the artist for an hour or half an hour of modeling--for rest, and for the first effort to transfer to the plastic clay some fleeting transient dream.

Meta Warrick Fuller was born in Philadelphia, Pennsylvania, June 9, 1877. For four years she attended the Pennsylvania School of Industrial Art, and it was at this institution that she first began to force serious recognition of her talent. Before very long she began to be known as a sculptor of the horrible, one of her first original pieces being a head of Medusa, with a hanging jaw, beads of gore, and eyes starting from their sockets. At her graduation in 1898 she won a prize for metal work by a crucifix upon which hung the figure of Christ in agony, and she also won honorable mention for her work in modeling. In a post-graduate year she won a much coveted prize in modeling. In 1899 Meta Warrick (then best known by her full name, Meta Vaux Warrick) went to Paris, where she worked and studied three years. Her work brought her in contact with many other artists, among them Augustus St. Gaudens, the sculptor of the Robert Gould Shaw Monument at the head of Boston Common. Then there came a day when by appointment the young woman went to see Auguste Rodin, who after years of struggle and dispraise had finally won recognition as the foremost sculptor in France if not in the world. The great man glanced one after another at the pieces that were presented to him, without very evident interest. At length, thrilled by the figure in "Silent Sorrow," sometimes referred to as "Man Eating His Heart Out," Rodin beamed upon the young woman and said, "Mademoiselle, you are a sculptor; you have the sense of form." With encouragement from such a source the young artist worked with renewed vigor, looking forward to the time when something that she had produced should win a place in the Salon, the great national gallery in Paris. "The Wretched," one of the artist's masterpieces, was exhibited here in 1903, and along with it went "The Impenitent Thief."

This latter production was demolished in 1904, after meeting with various unhappy accidents. In the form as presented, however, the thief, heroic in size, hung on the cross torn by anguish. Hardened, unsympathetic, and even defiant, he still possessed some admirable qualities of strength, and he has remained one of the sculptor's most powerful conceptions. In "The Wretched" seven figures greet the eye. Each represents a different form of human anguish. An old man, worn by hunger and disease, waits for death. A mother yearns for the loved ones she has lost. A man bowed by shame fears to look upon his fellow-creatures. A sick child suffers from some hereditary taint. A youth is in despair, and a woman is crazed by sorrow. Over all is the Philosopher who suffers perhaps more keenly than the others as he views the misery around them, and who, powerless to relieve it, also sinks into despair.

Other early productions were similarly characterized by a strongly romantic quality. "Silent Sorrow" has already been remarked in passing. In this a man, worn and gaunt and in despair, is represented as leaning over and actually eating out his own heart. "Man Carrying Dead Body" is in similar vein. The sculptor is moved by the thought of one who will be spurred on by the impulse of duty to the performance of some task not only unpleasant but even loathsome. She shows a man bearing across his shoulder the body of a comrade that has evidently lain on the battlefield for days. The thing is horrible, and the man totters under the great weight; but he forces his way onward until he can give it decent burial. Another early production was based on the ancient Greek story of Oedipus. This story was somewhat as follows: Oedipus was the son of Laius and Jocasta, king and queen of Thebes. At his birth an oracle foretold that the father Laius would be killed by his son. The child was sent away to be killed by exposure, but in course of time was saved and afterwards adopted by the King of Corinth. When he was grown, being warned by an oracle that he would kill his father and marry his mother, he left home. On his journey he met Laius and slew him in the course of an altercation. Later, by solving the riddle of the sphinx, he freed Thebes from distress, was made king of the city, and married Jocasta. Eventually the terrible truth of the relationship became known to all. Jocasta hanged herself and Oedipus tore out his eyes. The sculptor portrays the hero of the old legend at the very moment that he is thus trying to punish himself for his crime. There is nothing delicate or pretty about all such work as this. It is grewsome in fact, and horrible; but it is also strong and intense and vital. Its merit was at once recognized by the French, and it gave Meta Warrick a recognized place among the sculptors of America.

On her return to America the artist resumed her studies at the School of Industrial Art, winning in 1904 the Battles first prize for pottery. In 1907 she produced a series of tableaux representing the advance of the Negro for the Jamestown Tercentennial Exposition, and in 1913 a group for the New York State Emancipation Proclamation Commission. In 1909 she became the wife of Dr. Solomon C. Fuller, of Framingham, Massachusetts. A fire in 1910 unfortunately destroyed some of her most valuable pieces while they were in storage in Philadelphia. Only a few examples of her early work, that happened to be elsewhere, were saved. The artist was undaunted, however, and by May, 1914, she had sufficiently recovered from the blow to be able to hold at her home a public exhibition of her work.

After this fire a new note crept into the work of Meta Warrick Fuller. This was doubtless due not so much to the fire itself as to the larger conception of life that now came to the sculptor with the new duties of marriage and motherhood. From this time forth it was not so much the romantic as the social note that was emphasized. Representative of the new influence was the second model of the group for the Emancipation Proclamation Commission. A recently emancipated Negro youth and maiden stand beneath a gnarled, decapitated tree that has what looks almost like a human hand stretched over them. Humanity is pushing them forth into the world while at the same time the hand of Destiny is restraining them in the full exercise of their freedom. "Immigrant in America" is in somewhat similar vein. An American woman, the mother of one strong healthy child, is shown welcoming to the land of plenty the foreigner, the mother of several poorly nourished children. Closely related in subject is the smaller piece, "The Silent Appeal," in which a mother capable of producing and caring for three sturdy children is shown as making a quiet demand for the suffrage and for any other privileges to which a human being is entitled. All of these productions are clear cut, straightforward, and dignified.

In May, 1917, Meta Warrick Fuller took second prize in a competition under the auspices of the Massachusetts Branch of the Woman's Peace Party, her subject being "Peace Halting the Ruthlessness of War." War is personified as on a mighty steed and trampling to death numberless human beings. In one hand he holds a spear on which he has transfixed the head of one of his victims. As he goes on his masterful career Peace meets him and commands him to cease his ravages. The work as exhibited was in gray-green wax and was a production of most unusual spirit.

Among other prominent titles are "Watching for Dawn," a conception of remarkable beauty and yearning, and "Mother and Child." An early production somewhat detached from other pieces is a head of John the Baptist. This is one of the most haunting creations of Mrs. Fuller. In it she was especially successful in the infinite yearning and pathos that she somehow managed to give to the eyes of the seer. It bears the unmistakable stamp of power.

In this whole review of this sculptor's work we have indicated only the chief titles. She is an indefatigable worker and has produced numerous smaller pieces, many of these being naturally for commercial purposes. As has been remarked, while her work was at first romantic and often even horrible, in recent years she has been interested rather in social themes. There are those, however, who hope that she will not utterly forsake the field in which she first became distinguished. Through the sternness of her early work speaks the very tragedy of the Negro race. In any case It Is pleasant to record that the foremost sculptor of the race is not only an artist of rank but also a woman who knows and appreciates in the highest possible manner the virtues and the beauties of the home.

FOOTNOTE:

[B] For the further pursuit of this and related subjects the attention of the reader is invited to the author's "The Negro in Literature and Art" (Duffield & Co., New York, N. Y., 1918).

V.

MARY McLEOD BETHUNE

On October 3, 1904, a lone woman, inspired by the desire to do something for the needy ones of her race and state, began at Daytona, Florida, a training school for Negro girls. She had only one dollar and a half in money, but she had faith, energy, and a heart full of love for her people. To-day she has an institution worth not less than one hundred thousand dollars, with plans for extensive and immediate enlargement, and her school is one of the best conducted and most clear-visioned in the country. Such has been the result of boundless energy and thrift joined to an unwavering faith in God.

Mary McLeod was born July 10, 1875, in a three-room log cabin on a little cotton and rice farm about three miles from Mayesville, South Carolina, being one in the large family of Samuel and Patsy McLeod. Ambitious even from her early years, she yearned for larger and finer things than her environment afforded; and yet even the life that she saw around her was to prove a blessing in disguise, as it gave to her deeper and clearer insight into the problems, the shortcomings, and the needs of her people. In course of time she attended a little mission school in Mayesville, and she was converted at the age of twelve. Later she was graduated at Scotia Seminary, Concord, North Carolina, and then she went to the Moody Bible Institute in Chicago. In the years of her schooling she received some assistance from a scholarship given by Miss Mary Chrisman, a dressmaker of Denver, Colorado. Mary McLeod never forgot that she had been helped by a working woman. Some day she intended to justify that faith, and time has shown that never was a scholarship invested to better advantage.

In 1898 Mary McLeod was married. She became the mother of one son. Not long after, the family moved to Palatka, Florida. Now followed the hard years of waiting, of praying, of hoping; but through it all the earnest woman never lost faith in herself, nor in God. She gained experience in a little school that she taught, she sang with unusual effect in the churches of the town, and she took part in any forward movement or uplift enterprise that she could. All the while, however, she knew that the big task was yet to come. She prayed, and hoped, and waited.

By the fall of 1904 it seemed that the time had come. In a little rented house, with five girls, Mrs. Bethune began what is now the Daytona Normal and Industrial Institute for Negro Girls. By means of concerts and festivals the first payment of five dollars was made on the present site, then an old dump-pile. With their own hands the teacher and the pupils cleared away much of the rubbish, and from the first they invited the co-operation of the people around them by lending a helping hand in any way they could, by "being neighborly." In 1905 a Board of Trustees was organized and the school was chartered. In 1907 Faith Hall, a four-story frame house, forty by fifty feet, was "prayed up, sung up, and talked up;" and we can understand at what a premium space was in the earlier days when we know that this building furnished dormitory accommodations for teachers and students, dining-room, reading room, storerooms, and bathrooms. To the rear of Faith Hall was placed a two-story structure containing the school kitchen and the domestic science room. In 1909 the school found it necessary to acquire a farm for the raising of live stock and vegetables and for the practical outdoor training of the girls. After six weeks of earnest work the twelve-acre tract in front of the school was purchased. In 1914 a Model Home was built. In this year also an additional west farm of six acres, on which was a two-story frame building, was needed, asked for and procured. In March, 1918, the labors of fourteen years were crowned by the erection and dedication of a spacious auditorium; and among the speakers at the dedication were the Governor of Florida and the Vice-President of the United States. Efforts now look forward to a great new dormitory for the girls.

Such a bare account of achievements, however, by no means gives one an adequate conception of the striving and the hopings and the praying that have entered into the work. To begin with, Daytona was a strategic place for the school. There was no other such school along the entire east coast of Florida, and as a place of unusual beauty and attractiveness the town was visited throughout the winter by wealthy tourists. From the very first, however, the girls were trained in the virtues of the home, and in self-help. Great emphasis was placed on domestic science, and not only for this as an end in itself, but also as a means for the larger training in cleanliness and thrift and good taste. "We notice strawberries are selling at fifty and sixty cents a quart," said a visitor, "and you have a splendid patch. Do you use them for your students or sell them?" "We never eat a quart when we can get fifty cents for them," was the reply. "We can take fifty cents and buy a bone that will make soup for us all, when a quart of berries would supply only a few."

For one interested in education few pictures could be more beautiful than that of the dining-room at the school in the morning of a day in midterm. Florida is warm often even in midwinter; nevertheless, rising at five gives one a keen appetite for the early breakfast. The ceiling is low and there are other obvious disadvantages; but over all is the spirit of good cheer and of home. The tablecloths are very white and clean; flowers are on the different tables; at the head of each a teacher presides over five or six girls; the food is nourishing and well-prepared; and one leaves with the feeling that if he had a sister or daughter he would like for her to have the training of some such place as this.

Of such quality is the work that has been built up; and all has been accomplished through the remarkable personality of the woman who is the head and the soul of every effort. Indomitable courage, boundless energy, fine tact and a sense of the fitness of things, kindly spirit, and firm faith in God have deservedly given her success. Beyond the bounds of her immediate institution her influence extends. About the year 1912 the trustees felt the need of so extending the work as to make the school something of a community center; and thus arose the McLeod Hospital and Training School for Nurses. In 1912, moved by the utter neglect of the children of the turpentine camp at Tomoka, Mrs. Bethune started work for them in a little house that she secured. The aim was to teach the children to be clean and truthful and helpful, to sew and to sweep and to sing. A short school term was started among them, and the mission serves as an excellent practice school for the girls of the senior class in the Training School. A summer school and a playground have also been started for the children in Daytona. Nor have the boys and young men been neglected. Here was a problem of unusual difficulty. Any one who has looked into the inner life of the small towns of Florida could not fail to be impressed by the situation of the boys and young men. Hotel life, a shifting tourist population, and a climate of unusual seductiveness, have all left their impress. On every side to the young man beckons temptation, and in town after town one finds not one decent recreation center or uplifting social influence. Pool-rooms abound, and the young man is blamed for entering forbidden paths; but all too often the Christian men and women of the community have put forth no definite organized effort for his uplift. All too often there results a blasted life--a heartache for a mother, or a ruined home for some young woman. In Daytona, in 1913, on a lot near the school campus, one of the trustees, Mr. George S. Doane, erected a neat, commodious building to be used in connection with the extension work of the institution as a general reading-room and home for the Young Men's Christian Association; and this is the only specific work so being done for Negro boys in this section of the state. A debating club, an athletic club, lecture club, and prayer-meetings all serve as means toward the physical, intellectual, and spiritual development of the young men. A "Better Boys Movement" is also making progress and the younger boys are becoming interested in canning and farming as well as being cared for in their sports and games.

No sketch of this woman's work should close without mention of her activities for the nation at large. Red Cross work or a Liberty Loan drive has alike called forth her interest and her energy. She has appeared on some great occasions and before distinguished audiences, such as that for instance in the Belasco Theatre in Washington in December, 1917, when on a noteworthy patriotic occasion she was the only representative of her race to speak.

Her girls have gone into many spheres of life and have regularly made themselves useful and desirable. Nearly two hundred are now annually enrolled at the school. The demand for them as teachers, seamstresses, or cooks far exceeds the supply. In great homes and humble, in country or in town, in Daytona or elsewhere--North, South, East, West--they remember the motto of their teacher and of the Master of all, "Not to be ministered unto but to minister;" and year after year they accomplish better and better things for the school that they love so well and through it for the Kingdom of God.

* * * * *

Two thousand years ago the Savior of Mankind walked upon the earth, a man of sorrows and acquainted with grief; and the people hid as it were their faces from him. But one day he went into the home of a Pharisee and sat him down to meat. And a woman of the city, when she knew that Jesus sat at meat in the Pharisee's house, brought an alabaster box of ointment, exceeding precious, and began to wash his feet with her tears, and did wipe them with the hairs of her head, and kissed his feet, and anointed them with the ointment. And there were some that had indignation among themselves, and said, Why was this waste of the ointment made? But Jesus said, Let her alone. She hath wrought a good work on me. She hath done what she could. Verily, I say unto you, Wheresoever this gospel shall be preached throughout the whole world, this also that she hath done shall be spoken of for a memorial of her.

To-day as well as centuries ago the Christ is before us, around us, waiting. We do not always know him, for he appears in disguise, as a little orphan, or a sick old woman, or even perhaps as some one of high estate but in need of prayer. Let us do what we can. Let each one prove herself an earnest follower. To such end is the effort of Mary McLeod Bethune; and as we think of all that she has done and is doing let us for our own selves once more recall the beautiful words of Sister Moore: "There is no place too lowly or dark for our feet to enter, and no place so high and bright but it needs the touch of the light that we carry from the Cross."

VI.

MARY CHURCH TERRELL

With the increasingly complex problems of American civilization, woman is being called on in ways before undreamed of to bear a share in great public burdens. The recent great war has demonstrated anew the part that she is to play in our factories, our relief work, our religious organizations--in all the activities of our social and industrial life. The broadening basis of the suffrage in some states and the election of a woman to a seat in Congress have also emphasized the fact that in the new day woman as well as man will have to bear the larger responsibilities of citizenship. In all this intense life the Negro woman has taken a part, and she will have to do still more in the future. Even before the Civil War there were women of the race who labored, sometimes in large ways, for the influencing of sentiment and the salvation of their people. In the present period of our country's history new problems arise, sometimes even more delicate than those that went before them and even more difficult of solution--problems of education, readjustment, and of the proper moulding of public opinion. They call for keen intelligence, broad information, rich culture, and the ability to meet men and women of other races and other countries on the broad plane of cosmopolitanism. In public life and in the higher graces of society no woman of the race has commanded more attention from the American and the international public than Mary Church Terrell.

The life of this woman is an example of the possibilities not only of Negro but of American womanhood. She has appeared on platforms with men and women of other races, sometimes sturdy opponents on public questions, and more than held her own. She has attended an international congress in Europe and surpassed all the other women from her country in her ability to address audiences in languages other than English. With all this she has never forgotten the religious impulse that is so strong in the heart of her people and that ultimately is to play so large a part in their advancement. One admirer of her culture has said, "She should be engaged to travel over the country as a model of good manners and good English."

Mary Church was born in Memphis, Tennessee, the daughter of Robert R. and Louisa Ayres Church. When she was yet very young her parents sent her to Ohio to be educated, and here she remained until she was graduated from the classical course in 1884. Then for two years she taught at Wilberforce University in Ohio, and for one year more in a high school in Washington. Desirous of broadening her attainments, however, she now went to Europe for a period of study and travel. She remained two years, spending the time in France, Switzerland, Germany, and Italy, generally improving herself in language. On her return she resumed her work in Washington, and she was offered the registrarship at Oberlin College, a distinct compliment coming as it did from an institution of such high standing. She declined the attractive position, however, because of her approaching marriage to Robert H. Terrell, a graduate of Harvard College and formerly principal of a high school in Washington, who was appointed to a judgeship in the District of Columbia by President Roosevelt.

Since her marriage Mrs. Terrell has written much on topics of general interest and from time to time has formally appeared as a public lecturer. One of her strongest articles was that on Lynching in the North American Review for June, 1904. The centenary of the birth of Harriet Beecher Stowe in 1912 found her unusually well posted on the life and work of the novelist, so that after she lectured many times on the subject she brought together the results of her study in an excellent pamphlet. She was the first president of the National Association of Colored Women's Clubs, was twice re-elected, and, declining to serve further, was made honorary president for life. She was chosen as one of the speakers at the International Congress of Women held in Berlin in June, 1904. Said the Washington Post of her performance on this occasion: "The hit of the Congress on the part of the American delegates was made by Mrs. Mary Church Terrell of Washington, who delivered one speech in German and another in equally good French. Mrs. Terrell is a colored woman who appears to have been beyond every other of our delegates prominent for her ability to make addresses in other than her own language." In a letter to some of the largest newspapers in the country Mrs. Ida Husted Harper said further: "This achievement on the part of a colored woman, added to a fine appearance and the eloquence of her words, carried the audience by storm and she had to respond three times to the encores before they were satisfied. It was more than a personal triumph; it was a triumph for her race."

Mrs. Terrell has ever exhibited an intense interest in public affairs. On the occasion of the discharge of the Negro soldiers in Brownsville, Texas, in 1906, she at once comprehended the tremendous issues involved and by her interviews with men high in the nation's life did much for the improvement of a bad situation. When, some years ago, Congress by resolution granted power to the Commissioners of the District of Columbia to appoint two women upon the Board of Education for the public schools, Mrs. Terrell was one of the women appointed. She served on the Board for five years with signal ability and unusual success, and on the occasion of her resignation in 1912 was given a magnificent testimonial by her fellow-citizens.

It would be difficult to record all the different things that Mary Church Terrell has done or the numerous ways in which she has turned sentiment on the race problem. In recent years she has been drawn more and more to her own home. She is in constant demand as a speaker, however, and one or two experiences or incidents must not pass unremarked. In 1906 she was invited by Prof. Jeremiah W. Jenks to come to Cornell University to deliver her address on the Bright Side of the Race Problem. She was introduced by Prof. F. A. Fetter of the Department of Economics. When she had finished her lecture she was greeted by deafening applause, and then she was surrounded by an eager crowd desirous of receiving an introduction. One enthusiastic woman exclaimed, as she warmly shook the speaker's hand, "I was so glad to hear you say something about the bright side, and--do you know?--every Southern faculty woman was here." A little later she was the guest of honor at a reception in the home of Ex-Ambassador Andrew D. White, the first president of Cornell University.

Just what Mary Church Terrell means as an inspiration to the young women of the Negro race one might have seen some years ago if he could have been present at Spelman Seminary on the occasion of the twenty-fifth anniversary of this the largest school for Negro girls in the world. She was preceded on the program by one or two prominent speakers who tried to take a broad view of the race problem but who were plainly baffled when they came face to face with Southern prejudice. When Mrs. Terrell rose to speak the air was tense with eagerness and anxiety. How she acquitted herself on this occasion, how eloquently she plead, and how nimbly and delicately she met her opponents' arguments, will never be forgotten by any one who was privileged to hear her.

The compliments that have been paid to the eloquence, the grace, the culture, the tact, and the poise of this woman are endless. She exhibits exceptional attainments either on or off the platform. Her words bristle with earnestness and energy, quickly captivating an audience or holding the closest attention in conversation. Her gestures are frequent, but always in sympathetic harmony. Her face is inclined to be sad in repose, but lights quickly and effectively to the soul of whatever subject she touches. Her voice is singularly clear and free from harsh notes. She exhibits no apparent effort in speaking, and at once impresses an audience by her ease, her courage, and her self-abnegation. Through all her work moreover constantly thrills her great hope for the young men and women of her race, so many of whom she has personally inspired.

Such a woman is an asset to her country and an honor to the race to which she belongs.

###

Made in the USA
Las Vegas, NV
20 May 2024